Hush Dear Soul
Your Time is Near
A Lullaby for the Soul

by Cristina Carballo Perelman, M.D.

HUSH DEAR SOUL, YOUR TIME IS NEAR
A Lullaby for the Soul

by Cristina Carballo-Perelman, M.D.

Copyright 2015, Cristina Carballo-Perelman, M.D.

ALL RIGHTS RESERVED, NO PART OF THIS PUBLICATION MAY BE REPRODUCED OR TRANSMITTED IN ANY FORM OR BY ANY MEANS, ELECTRONIC OR MECHANICAL, INCLUDING PHOTOCOPY, RECORDING OR ANY INFORMATION STORAGE RETRIEVAL SYSTEM, WITHOUT PERMISSION IN WRITING FROM THE COPYRIGHT OWNER.

Illustrations and Cover design by Sebastian Carballo
Cover and Book layout by Suzanne Parrott

ISBN: 978-0-9967412-3-7 (pbk)
ISBN: 978-0-9984178-4-4 (hbk)
Library of Congress Control Number: 2015918245

Printed in the United States of America
Publisher: CCP Enterprises, LLC

DEDICATION

I dedicate this book to everyone who has either faced the death of a loved one, a pet or has been frightened of their own impending end of life.

I also dedicate it to all the hospice workers, nurses, physicians and healthcare workers that face the death of their patients, daily, with courage and grace.

I wrote this as a companion to my book, "The Caretaker of All Souls, An Intimate Interview with Death" and hope it will bring comfort to all who read this.

My inspiration was of course, Death, whispering into my Soul, the words needed to provide the reader comfort, during a time of sadness.

Please be free to read it to anyone in need of comforting words.

It can even be sung to the tune of *Hush Little Baby, Don't You Cry,* author unknown.

May the warmth, love, kindness and grace that Death brings, envelop all who are present and bring comfort to all.

Hush dear Soul, for I am near.
Don't fret, don't worry, please no tears.

Do not think of Me, Death, as dark and severe,
I am made of light and love, never fear.

Your Soul will be safe,
On the journey we take.

You will never feel the chill of night,
On My wings of pure warmth and light.

Hush dear Soul, for I am near.
Together we'll soar, for now I am here.

In many circles I am feared,
I wish instead I was held dear.

With respect and compassion, I do My work,
Not in darkness or despair do I lurk.

Hush dear Soul, please don't fight.
Together we'll soar on My wings of light.

I'll keep you so warm and safe,
Where we'll go will be no war or hate.

Hush dear Soul, for I am near.
Together we'll soar, for now I am here.

When you think of Me, think about the circle of life,
I bring new hope, no more pain or strife.

So make sure you enjoy each moment on earth,
Because where I'll take will be a re-birth.

Your Soul will be cleansed and be pure again,
You will understand when it's your time, dear friend.

Hush dear Soul, for I am near.
Together we'll soar, for now I am here.

If your Soul is sad from losing your pet,
You will be reunited, one day, don't fret.

For every animal you have loved through the years,
You have infused them with a part of your Soul, my dear.

So when that animal's Soul is released,
I'll keep it safe for you, it's no longer a beast.

When your Soul then comes with Me,
I bring you all together, as one to be free.

You will see your friends just as they once appeared,
And you'll be united forever more, never fear.

Hush dear Soul, for I am near.
Together we'll soar, for now I am here.

Babies that are born and die right away,
Others who decide to take their life one day,
I treat all these Souls with a great deal of care,
Give them compassion, love and hope in a world too harsh to bear.

Those that come with Me from a war no one wins,
Those that leave this world from sickness, not sins.

Those that choose to leave before the illness takes all,
Those that leave because Mother Nature calls.

All these Souls I take with Me,
With a great deal of love, I set them free.

Bring them to healing and hope they repair,
The broken dreams, it all seems so unfair.

Hush dear Soul, for I am near.
Together we'll soar, for now I am here.

And when the mind can no longer remember,
Full of confusion, fear and temper.

The Soul will separate from the physical
   and hover,
Until I come to assist with the other.

And though the body and mind will decay,
Never fear, the Soul will continue to relay,
The memories so dear, so precious from
   every day.

The Soul will never forget the love and joy it
   gave and was given,
That created its eternal flame that is so driven.

Hush dear Soul, for I am near,
Together we'll soar, for now I am here.

I must warn all who listen that I also take,
All the Souls that are so full of hate.
These Souls may not be able to be repaired,
They will not be allowed to cause more despair.

What will happen to them, you might implore?
These souls will be destroyed, forevermore.
As I take these Souls to the Higher Source,
They will feel the pain that they enforced.
They may feel they have a chance to repent,
Beg for mercy and be resent,
Back to this life to repay the debt.

But some of these Souls can never go back,
No amount of good deeds will negate that fact.
And so their energy will be released,
Back to the Universe, forever deceased.
This is just a warning, for others, not you.
Your Soul is full of love, this is true.
So hush dear Soul, for I am near.
Together we'll soar, for now I am here.

This is where I leave you for now, dear Soul,
My wish for you is simple, please let me extol.
I wish for you to understand and accept your fate,
    and never fear My visit, please don't hate.
Understand I will one day take your Soul to a
    better place,
Full of light, compassion, love and grace.
You will see your loved ones, all living things,
Your Souls will be united and they will sing.
The light of your Soul will join the Universe,
But also stay separate, so you can continue
    to serve.
For the Higher Source of the Universe and I are
    everywhere,
I give back the Souls to the Universe to continue
    to repair.

And in the future I will sing this lullaby into
    your ear,

Hush dear Soul, for I am near,
Together we'll soar, for now I am here.

And in the future I will sill this lullaby into yuor ear,

Hush dear Soul, for I am near,
Together we'll soar, for now I am here.